LATER ELEMENTARY

Christmas Creations

11 SEASONAL PIANO SOLOS

Arranged by RANDALL HARTSELL

ISBN 978-1-4234-8010-5

WILLIS MUSIC

EXCLUSIVELY DISTRIBUTED BY

HAL•LEONARD®
CORPORATION
7777 W. BLUEMOUND RD. P.O. BOX 13819 MILWAUKEE, WI 53213

Visit Hal Leonard Online at
www.halleonard.com

Angels We Have Heard on High

Traditional French Carol
Arranged by Randall Hartsell

Moderately

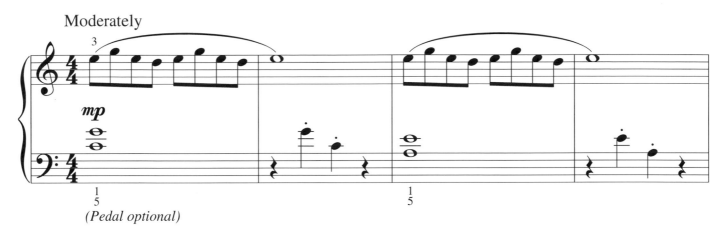

mp

(Pedal optional)

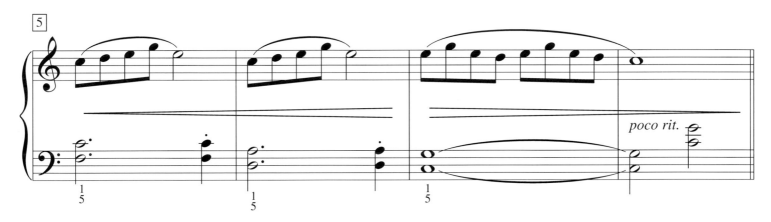

poco rit.

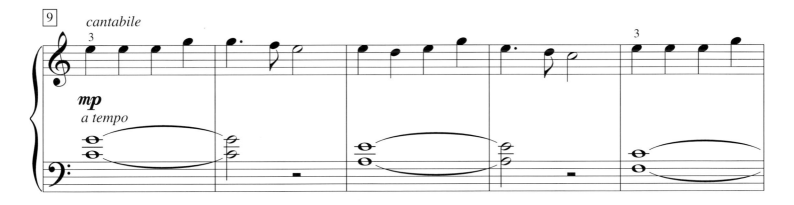

cantabile

mp
a tempo

mf

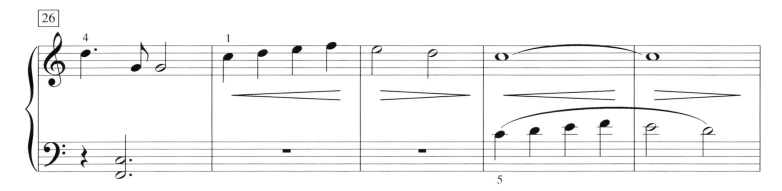

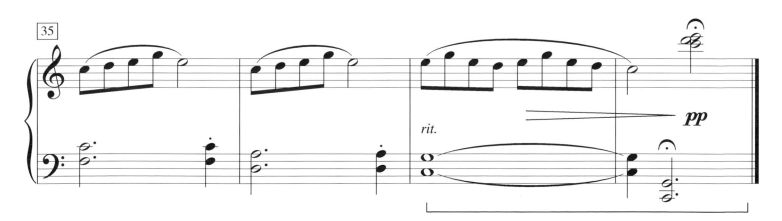

Away in a Manger

Music by James R. Murray
Arranged by Randall Hartsell

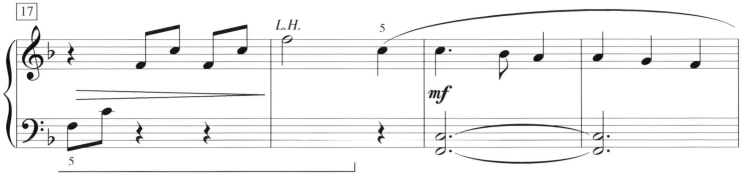

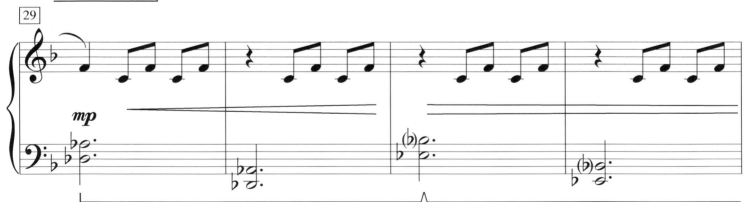

Carol of the Bells

Ukrainian Christmas Carol
Arranged by Randall Hartsell

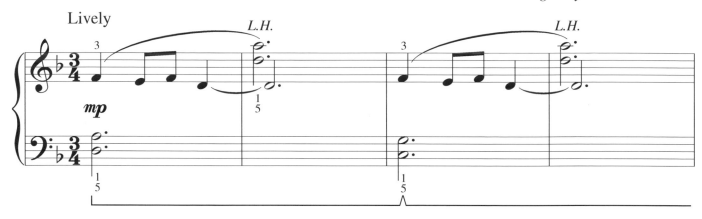

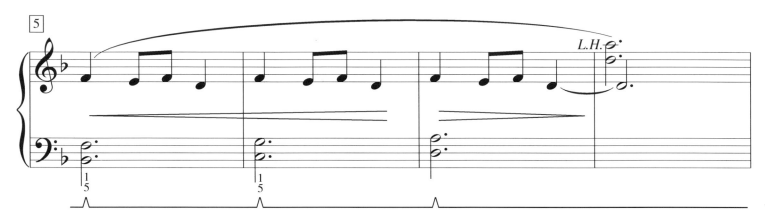

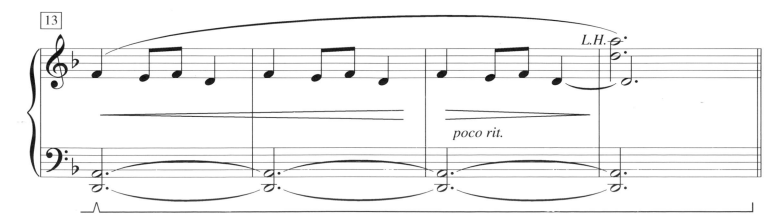

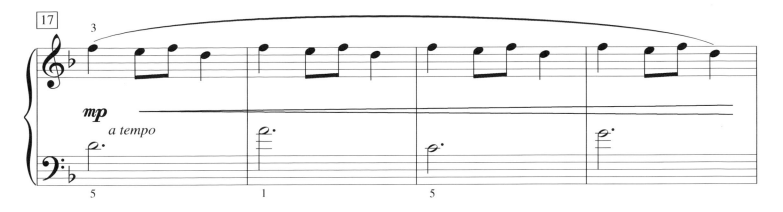

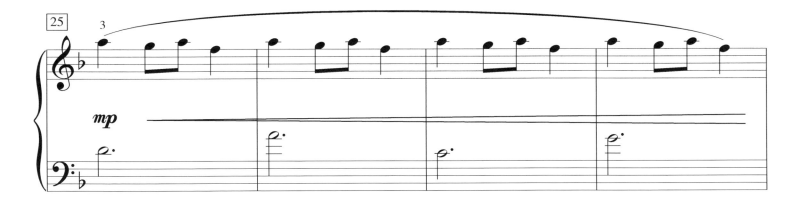

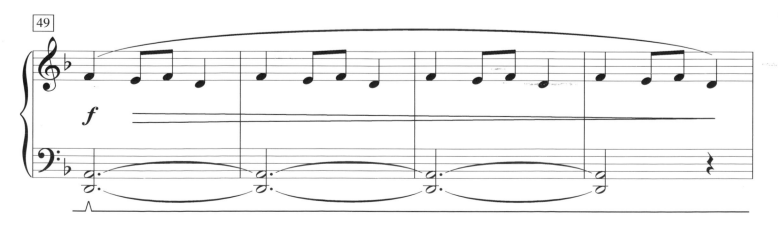

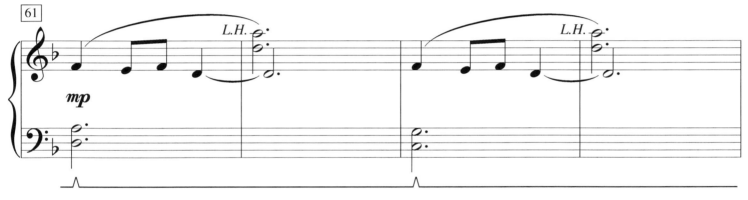

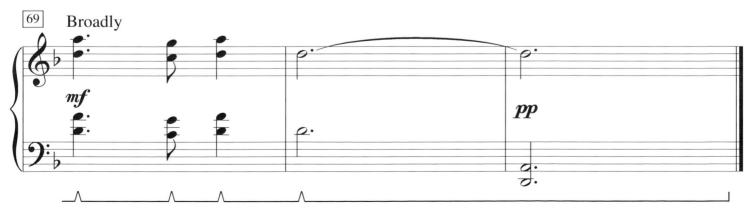

Deck the Hall

Traditional Welsh Carol
Arranged by Randall Hartsell

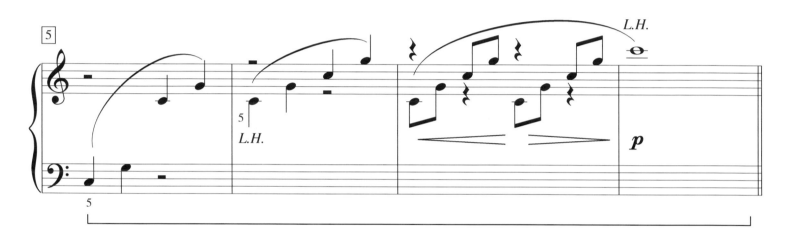

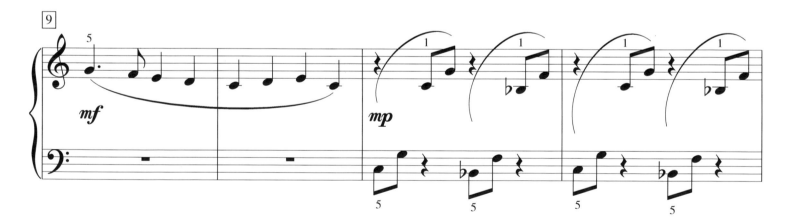

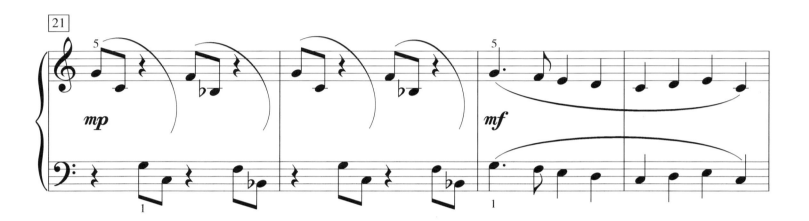

God Rest Ye Merry, Gentlemen

19th Century English Carol
Arranged by Randall Hartsell

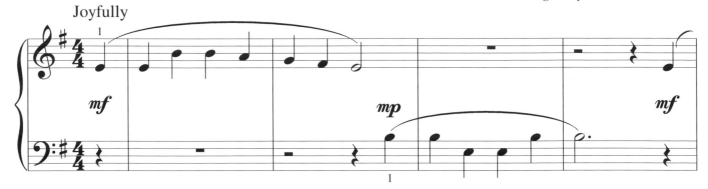

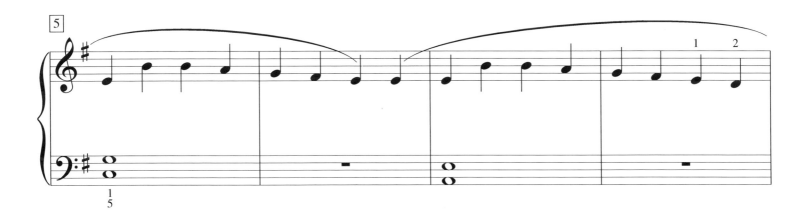

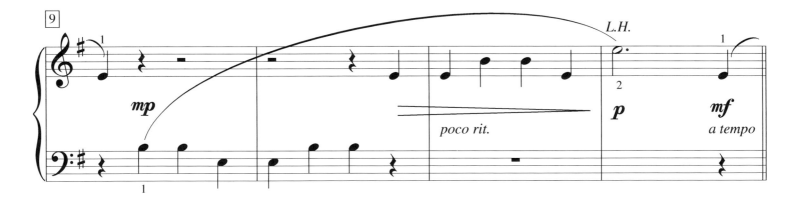

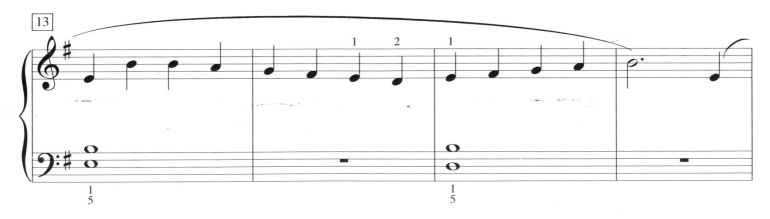

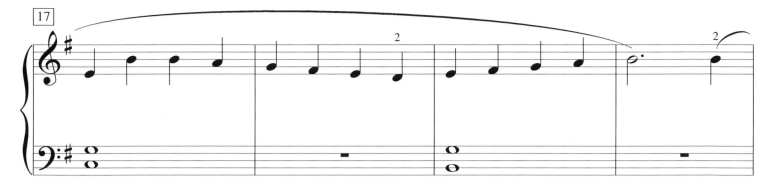

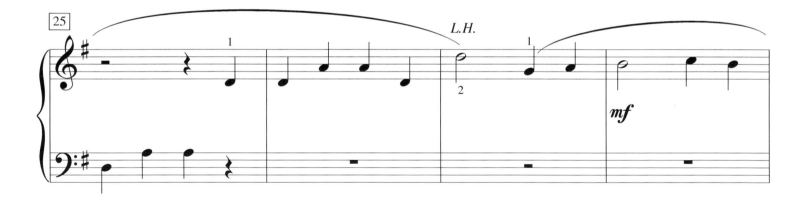

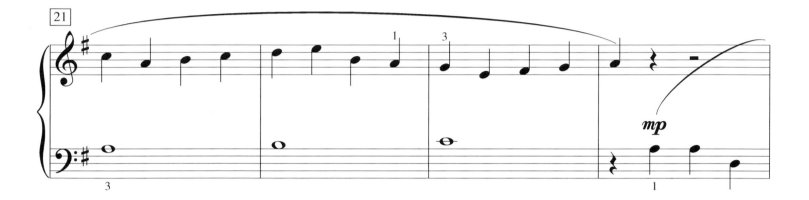

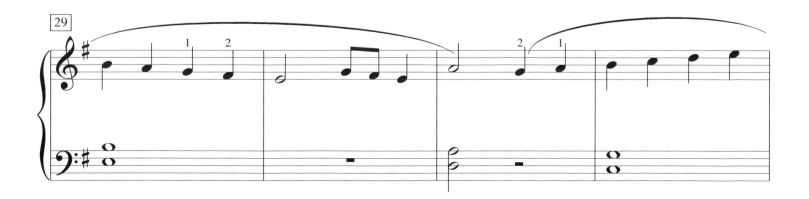

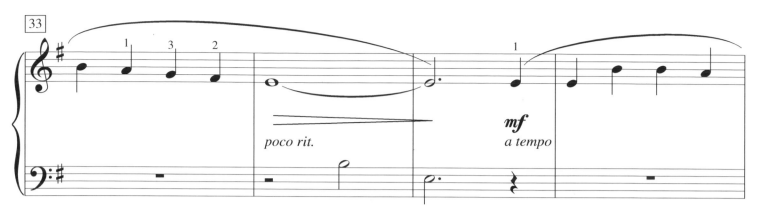

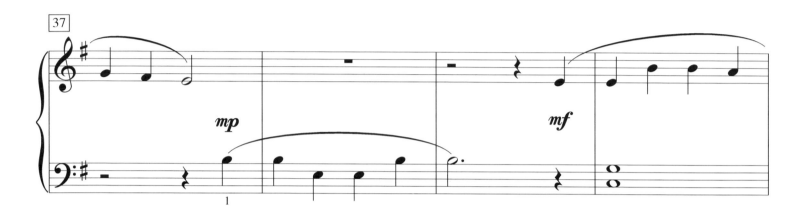

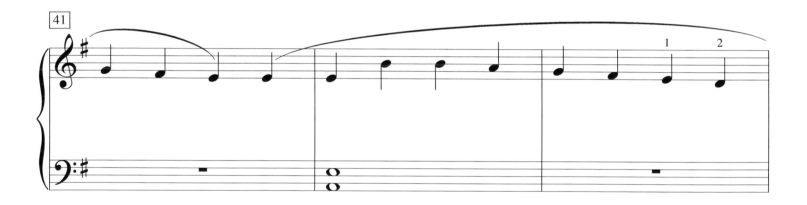

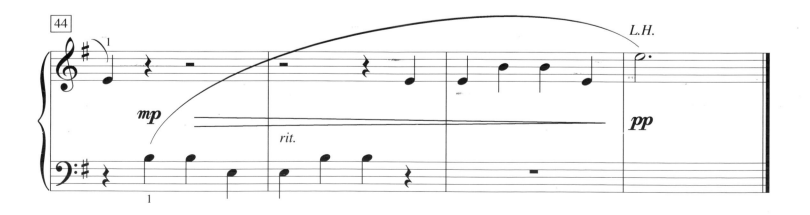

Good King Wenceslas

Words by John M. Neale
Music from *Piae Cantiones*
Arranged by Randall Hartsell

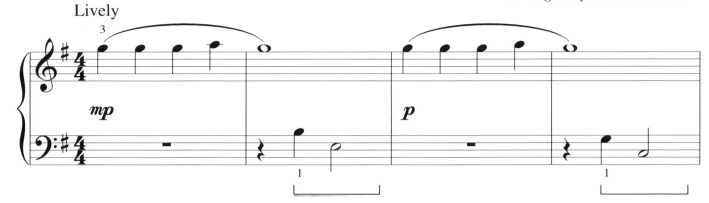

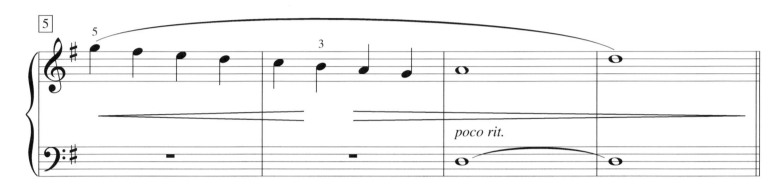

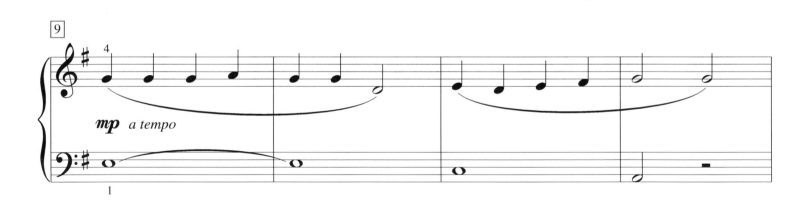

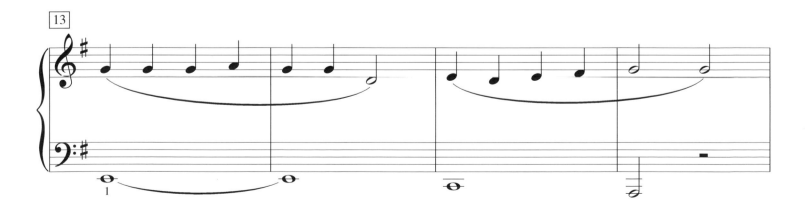

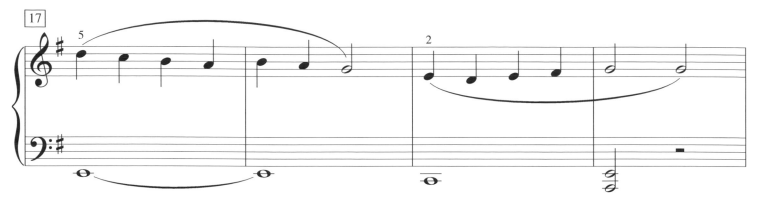

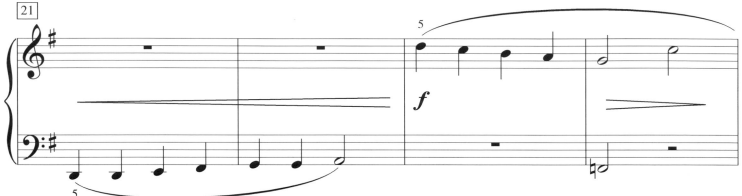

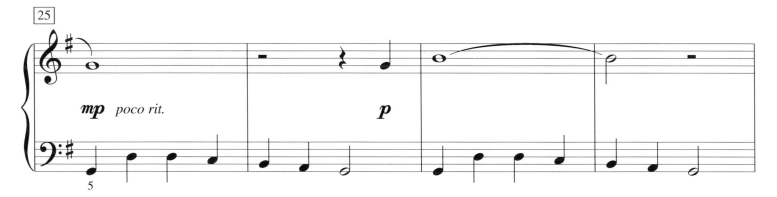

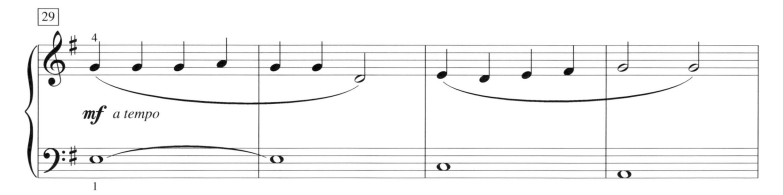

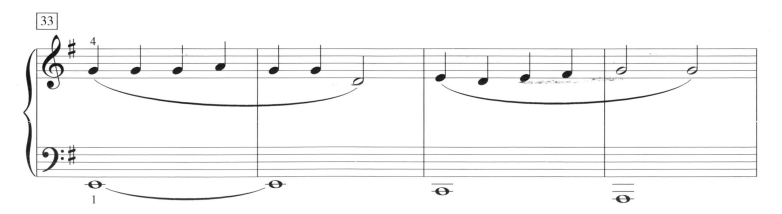

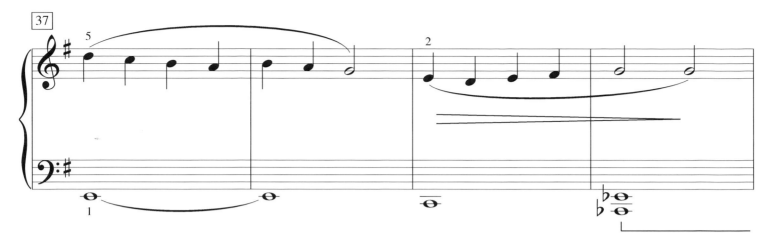

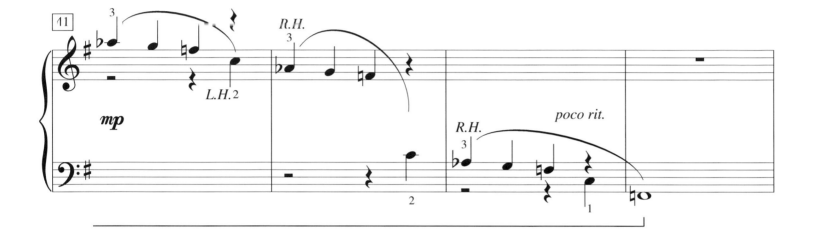

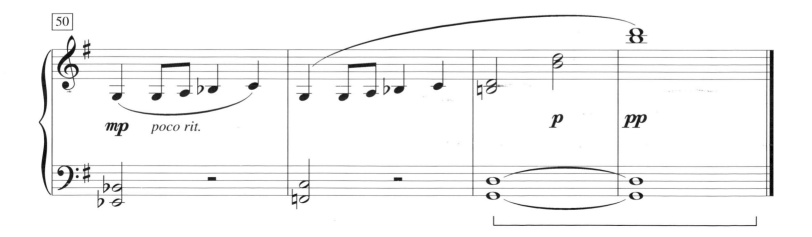

Jingle Bells

Words and Music by J. Pierpont
Arranged by Randall Hartsell

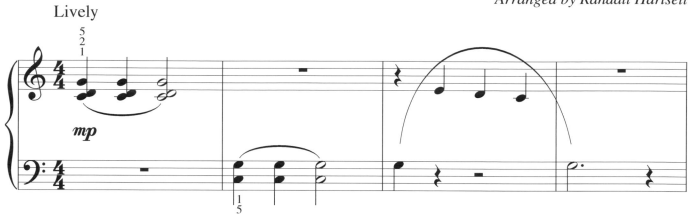

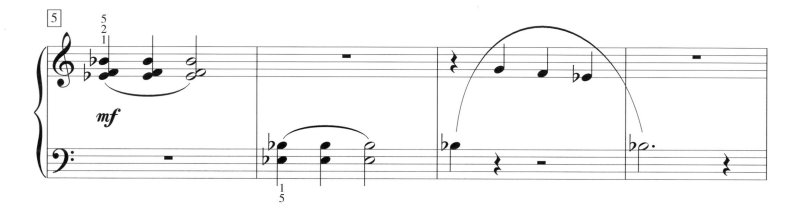

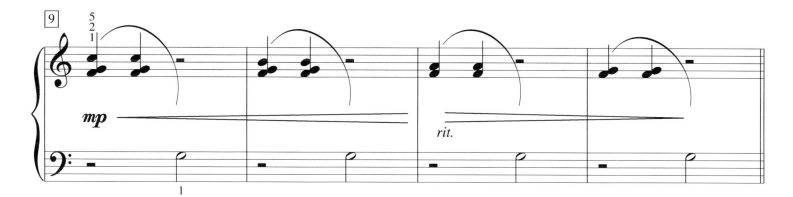

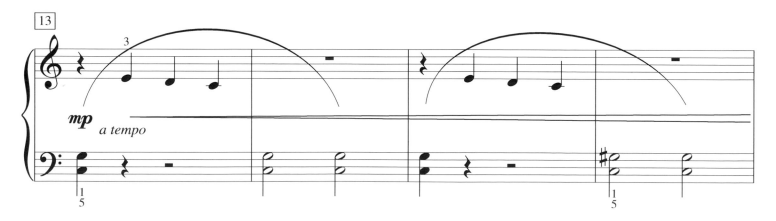

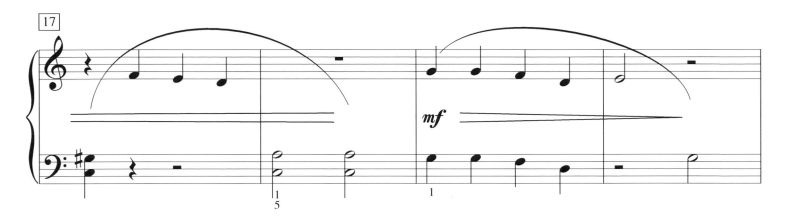

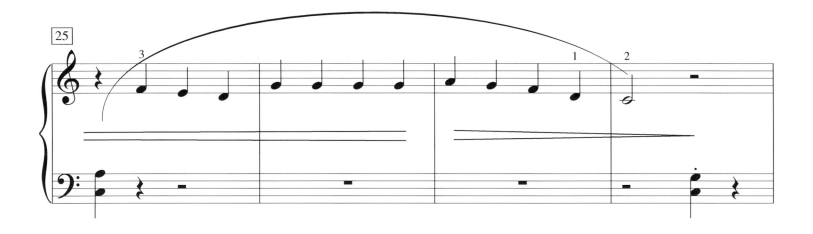

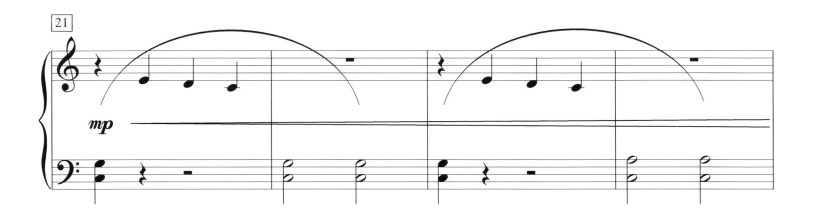

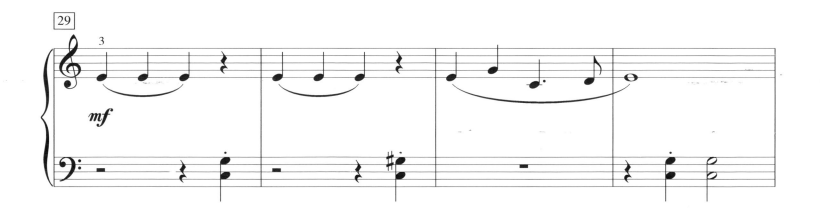

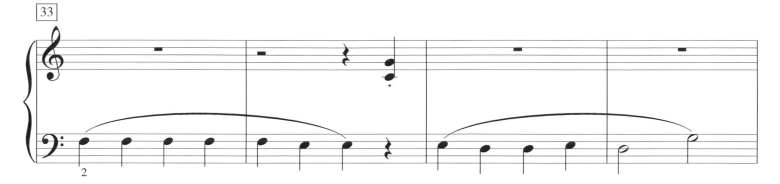

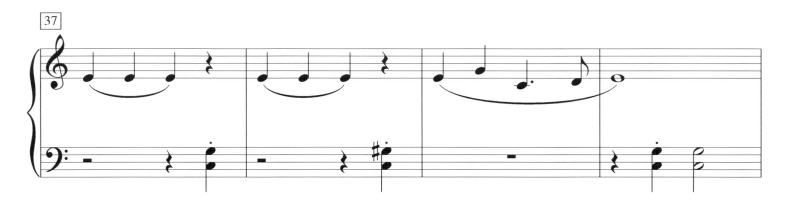

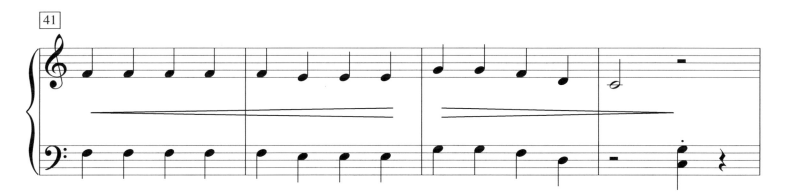

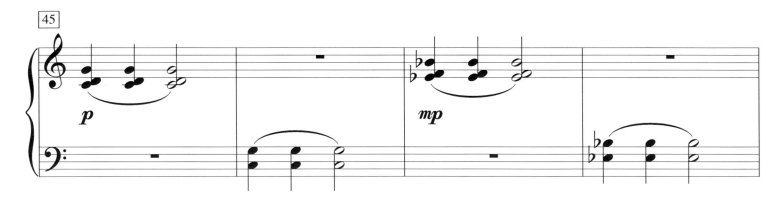

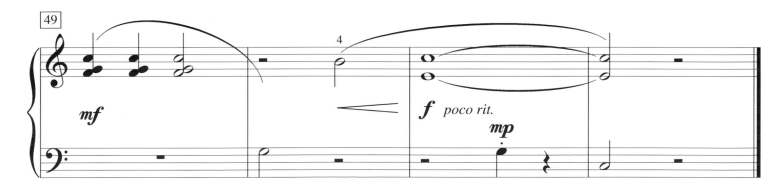

Joy to the World

Words by Isaac Watts
Music by George Frideric Handel
Adapted by Lowell Mason
Arranged by Randall Hartsell

Joyfully

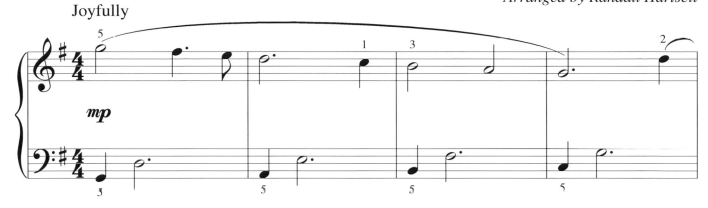

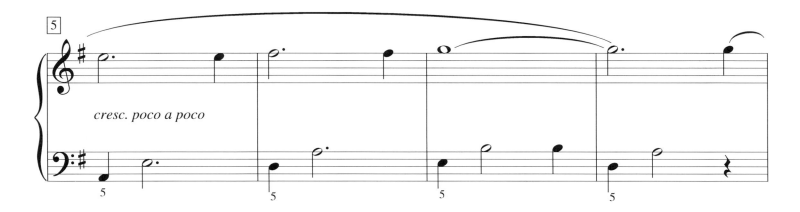

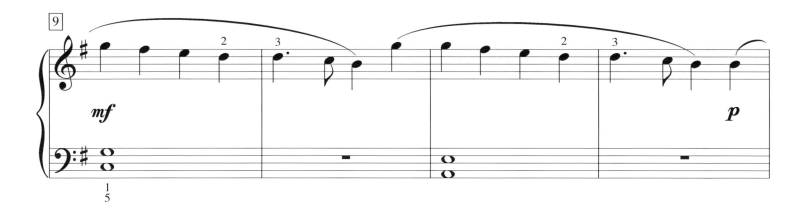

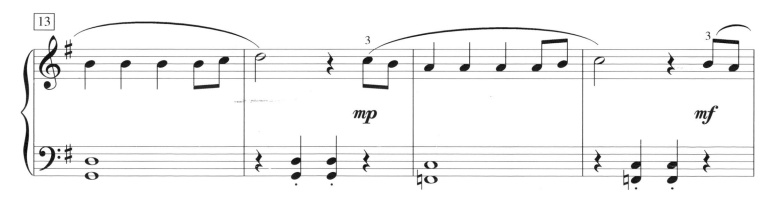

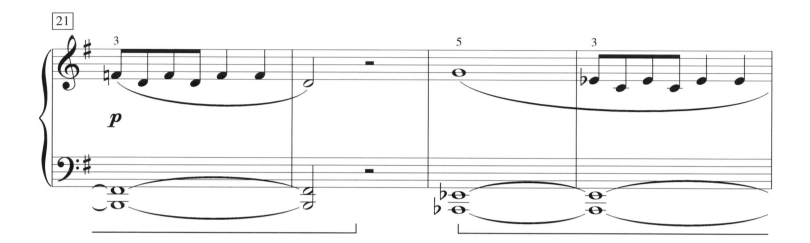

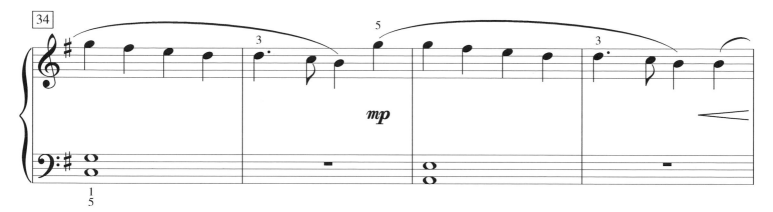

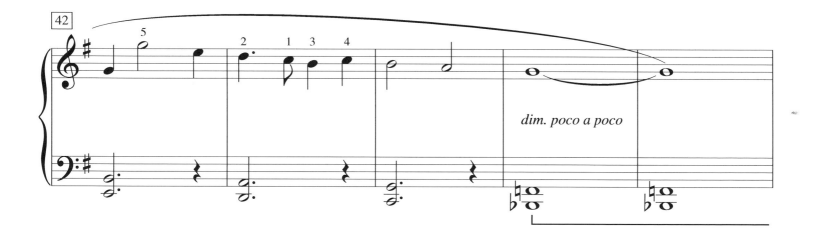

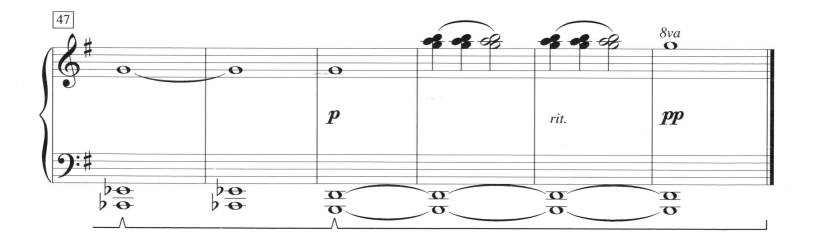

O Come, Little Children

Words by C. von Schmidt
Music by J.P.A. Schulz
Arranged by Randall Hartsell

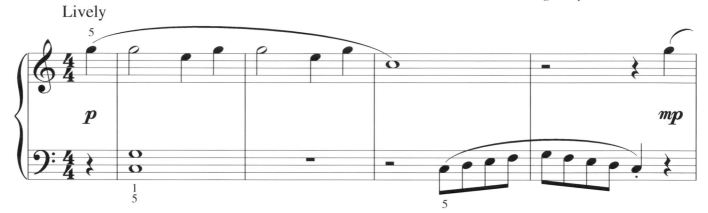

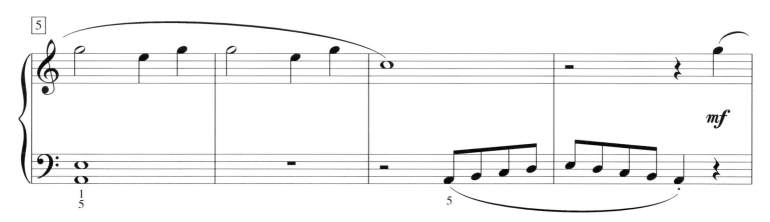

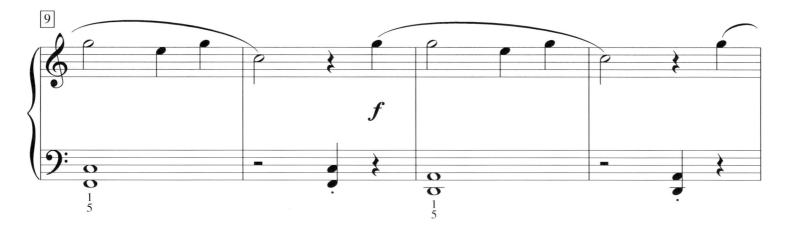

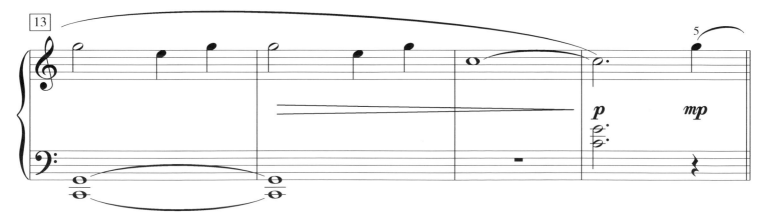

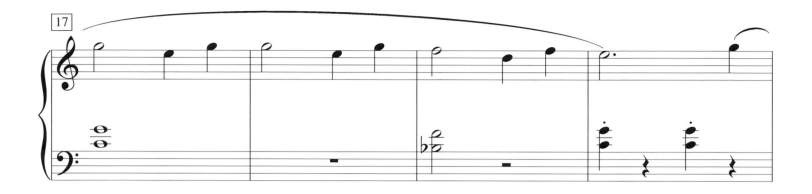

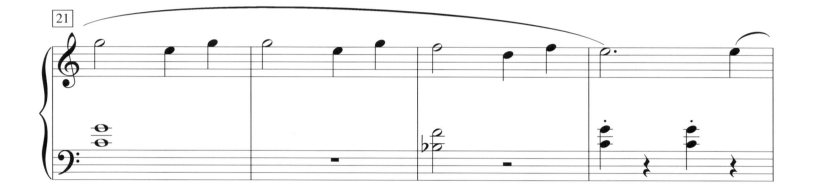

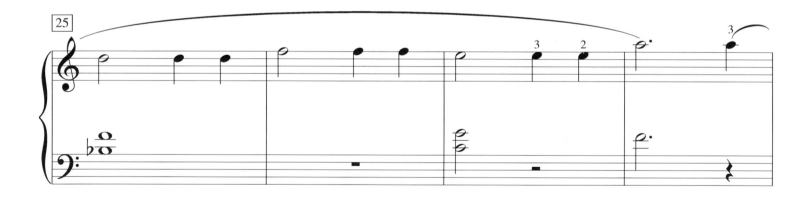

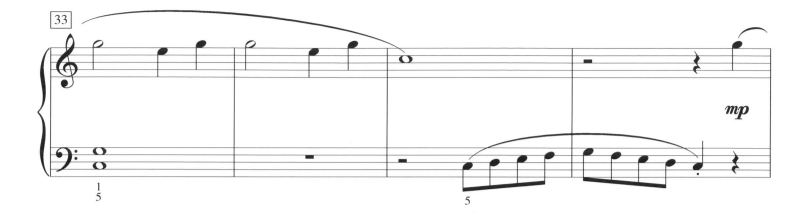

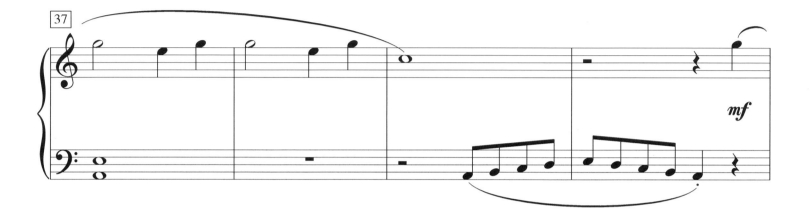

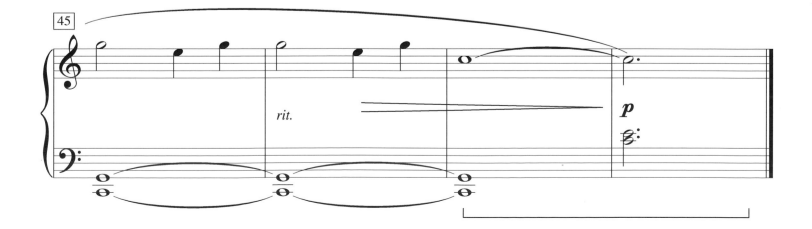

We Three Kings of Orient Are

Words and Music by John H. Hopkins, Jr.
Arranged by Randall Hartsell

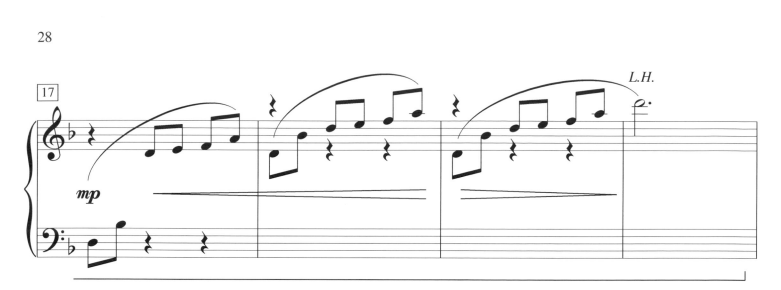

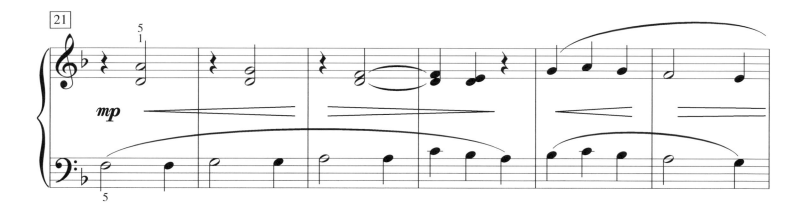

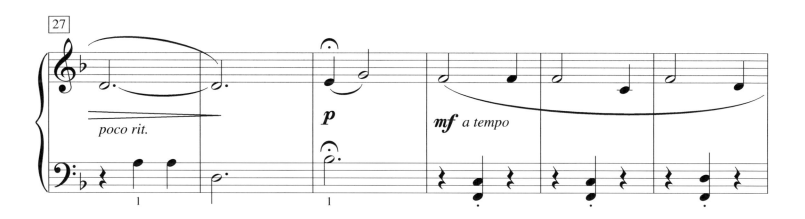

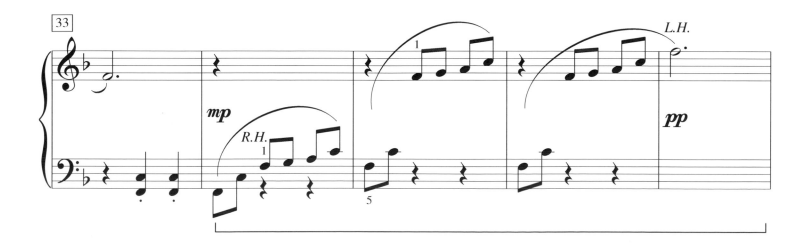

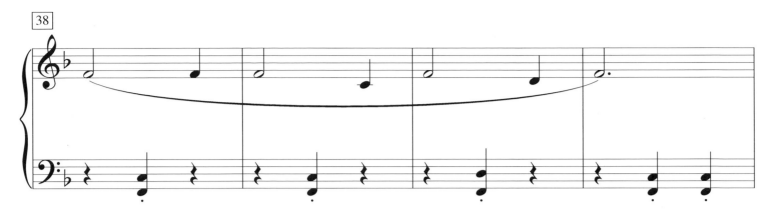

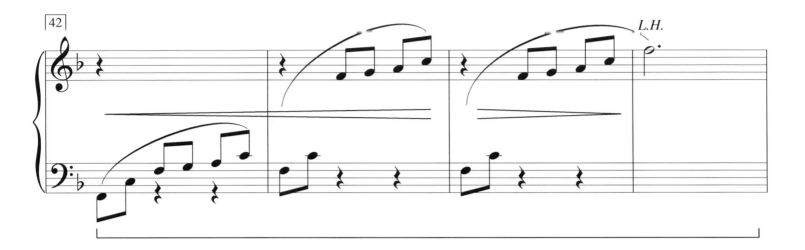

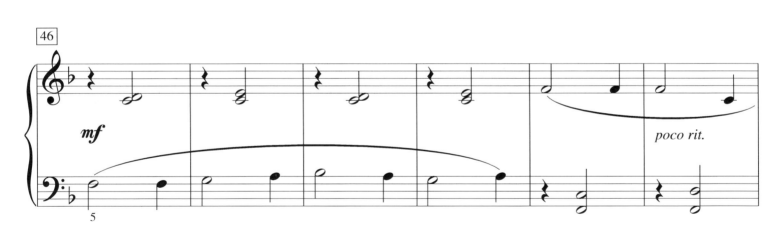

Silent Night

Words by Joseph Mohr
Translated by John F. Young
Music by Franz X. Gruber
Arranged by Randall Hartsell

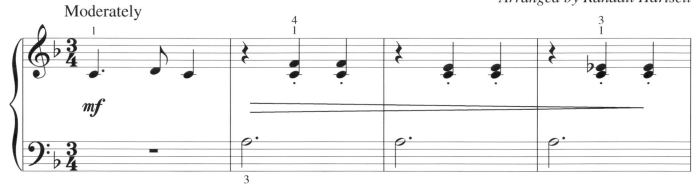

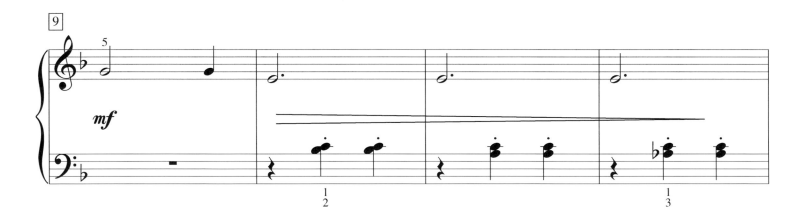

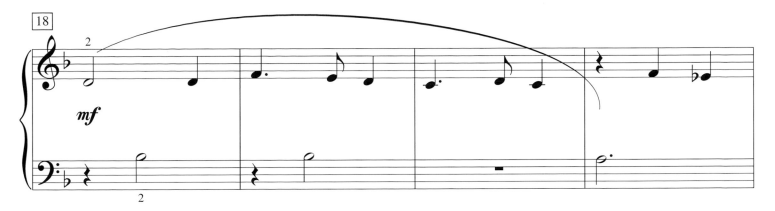

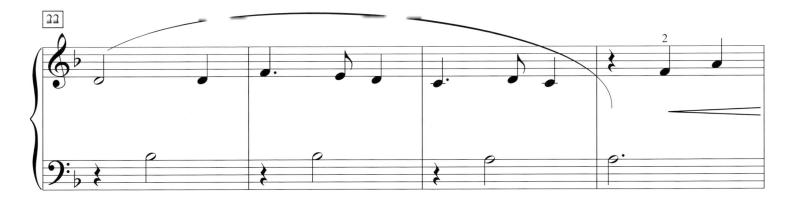

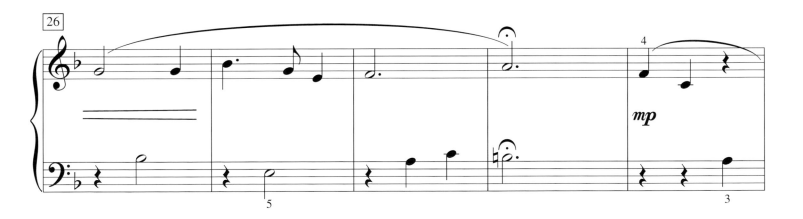

RANDALL HARTSELL is a composer, pianist/organist, clinician and teacher from Charlotte, North Carolina. Mr. Hartsell is particularly known for his lyrical and melodic compositional style, and consistently aims to write pieces that students will love to play and teachers will love to teach! He currently operates a private studio in the Charlotte area.

Mr. Hartsell is a graduate of East Carolina University, where he majored in piano pedagogy and performance, and was previously on the faculty of the school of music at the University of North Carolina (Charlotte). Mr. Hartsell currently has over 100 publications in print, and has also been featured as a commissioned composer in *Clavier* magazine.